Whales and Dolphins

KINGFISHER
LONDON & NEW YORK

Distributed in the U.S. by Macmillan, 175 Fifth Ave., New York, NY 10010
Distributed in Canada by H.B. Fenn and Company Ltd.,
34 Nixon Road, Bolton, Ontario L7E 1W2

First published as *Kingfisher Young Knowledge: Whales and Dolphins* in 2005
Additional material produced for Kingfisher by Discovery Books Ltd.

Library of Congress Cataloging-in-Publication data has been applied for.

ISBN 978-0-7534-6448-9

Kingfisher books are available for special promotions and premiums.
For details contact: Special Markets Department, Macmillan,
175 Fifth Avenue, New York, NY 10010.

For more information, please visit www.kingfisherbooks.com

Printed in China
10 9 8 7 6 5 4 3 2 1
1TR/0410/WKT/UNTD/140MA/C

Note to readers: the website addresses listed in this book are correct at
the time of going to print. However, due to the ever-changing nature
of the Internet, website addresses and content can change. Websites
can contain links that are unsuitable for children. The publisher cannot
be held responsible for changes in website addresses or content or
for information obtained through a third party. We strongly advise
that Internet searches be supervised by an adult.

Acknowledgments
The publishers would like to thank the following for permission to reproduce their material. Every care has been taken
to trace copyright holders. However, if there have been unintentional omissions or failure to trace copyright holders,
we apologize and will, if informed, endeavor to make corrections in any future edition.
b = bottom, *c* = center, *l* = left, *t* = top, *r* = right

Cover main Shutterstock/Kristian Skeulic; cover *l* Seapics/Masa Ushioda; cover *r* Seapics/James D. Watt; 1 Seapics/Masa Ushioda; 2–3 Getty/Taxi; 4–5 Nature pl/Brandon Cole;
6 Minden/Flip Nicklin; 7*t* Seapics/Armin Maywald; 7*b* Seapics/Doug Perrine; 8–9 Seapics/Doug Perrine; 8*b* Nature pl/Sue Flood; 9*b* Seapics/Ingrid Visser; 10 Minden/
Flip Nicklin; 11*t* Seapics/David B. Fleetham; 11*c* Seapics/Mark Conlin; 11*b* OSF/David Fleetham; 12*b* Seapics/Michael S. Nolan; 13*t* Minden/Mitsuaki Iwago; 14–15 Corbis/
Craig Tuttle; 15*t* Seapics/Doug Perrine; 15*r* Corbis/Lester V. Bergman; 15*b* Seapics/Doug Perrine; 16–17 Alamy; 17*t* Seapics/Hiroya Minakuchi; 17*b* Seapics/Masa Ushioda;
18–19 Seapics/Duncan Murrell; 19*t* Seapics/Philip Colla; 20–21 Minden/Flip Nicklin; 20*b* Ardea; 22–23 SeaQuest; 23*b* Seapics; 24–25 Minden/Flip Nicklin; 25*t* Seapics/Masa
Ushioda; 25*b* Seapics/Xavier Safont; 26*b* Seapics/Hiroya Minakuchi; 26–27 Seapics/Masa Ushioda; 27*t* Seapics/Robert L. Pitman; 28*b* Seapics/James D. Watt; 29*t* Seapics/Bob
Cranston; 30–31 Seapics/Doug Perrine; 31*t* Seapics/James D. Watt; 31*b* Seapics/Masa Ushioda; 32–33 Seapics; 32*b* Seapics/Hiroya Minakuchi; 33*t* Seapics/John K. B. Ford;
34 Minden/Flip Nicklin; 35*t* Corbis; 35*b* AA; 36–37 SeaQuest; 36*c* Corbis/Peter Turnley; 38–39 Seapics/Phillip Colla; 39*t* Minden/Flip Nicklin; 39*b* Minden/Flip Nicklin;
40–41 Minden/Mike Parry; 41 Corbis; 48*t* Shutterstock Images/Lars Christensen; 48*b* Shutterstock Images/CampCrazy Photography; 49*t* Shutterstock Images/
Ivan Cholakov Gostock-dot-net; 49*b* Shutterstock Images/J. Helgason; 52*c* Shutterstock Images/Kristian Sekulic; 52*b* Shutterstock Images/rm; 53*t* Shutterstock Images/
Karel Gallas; 56*b* Shutterstock Images/Steve Noakes

Illustrations: 12–13 Michael Langham Rowe; 23*t*, 28–29 Steve Weston
Commissioned photography on pages 42–47 by Andy Crawford. Thank you to models Lewis Manu, Adam Dyer, and Rebecca Roper

discover science

Whales and Dolphins

Caroline Harris

KINGFISHER
NEW YORK

Contents

What are whales and dolphins?

Whales and dolphins are mammals that live in water. They have warm blood and swim to the ocean's surface to breathe.

Baby care

A dolphin mother usually gives birth to one baby, called a calf, at a time. The newborn calf swims close to its mother's side for the first few weeks of its life.

Bristly faces

Most mammals are covered with hair or fur. This porpoise's skin is smooth, but young cetaceans (the name that scientists use for whales, dolphins, and porpoises) still have hairs on their faces.

Ripe old age

Dolphins can live to be 50 years old, while large whales, such as this southern right whale, may live to be 100!

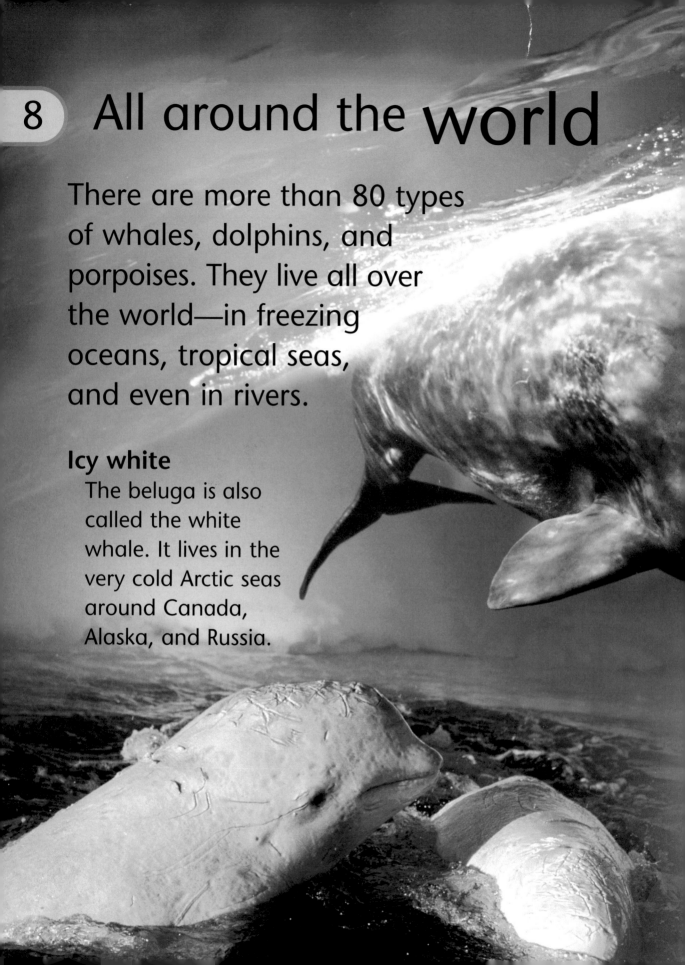

All around the world

There are more than 80 types of whales, dolphins, and porpoises. They live all over the world—in freezing oceans, tropical seas, and even in rivers.

Icy white

The beluga is also called the white whale. It lives in the very cold Arctic seas around Canada, Alaska, and Russia.

Whales everywhere

Sperm whales live in every ocean of the world. The females and young stay in tropical areas, while the males travel as far as the Arctic and Antarctica to feed.

Warm-water swimmer

The short-beaked common dolphin is found in many oceans and seas. It likes warm water, so it does not swim too far north or south.

Amazing creatures

Whales and dolphins come in some incredible shapes and sizes. Did you know that the largest animal on Earth is a whale?

Dolphin magic
The boto, or Amazon dolphin, is one of four species of dolphins that are found only in rivers. It is also called the pink dolphin because it has rose-colored skin.

Sea giant

The blue whale is the world's largest mammal. It can weigh 200 tons—the same as 32 elephants. A blue whale this huge has a heart the size of a car!

blue whale

skeleton of a blue whale

Water unicorn

The male narwhal has a tusk that can reach 10 feet (3 meters) long. Tales of unicorns may have begun when people first saw narwhal tusks.

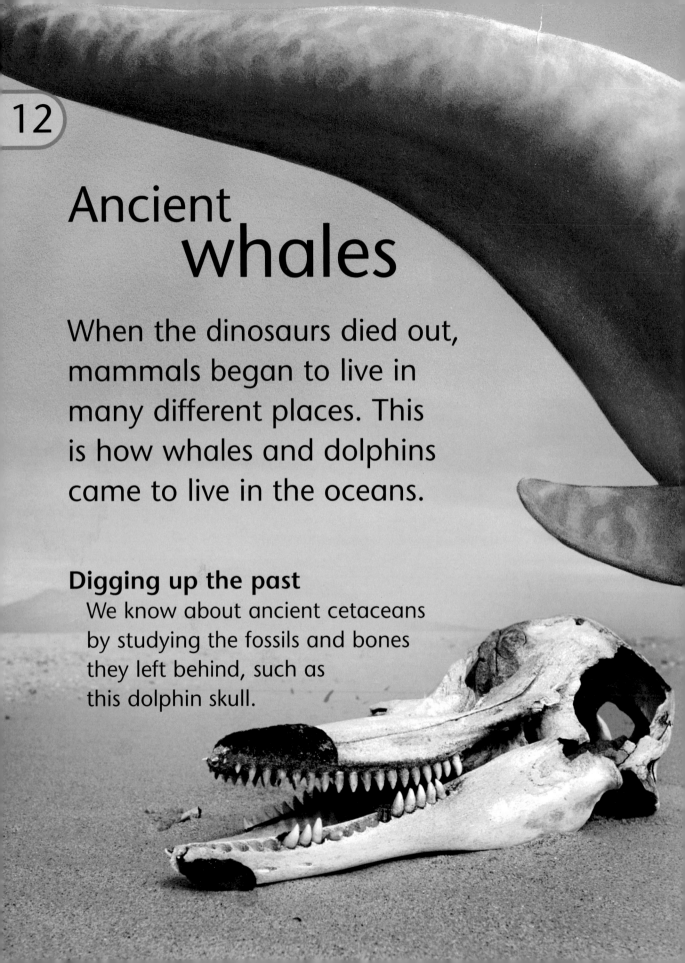

Ancient whales

When the dinosaurs died out, mammals began to live in many different places. This is how whales and dolphins came to live in the oceans.

Digging up the past

We know about ancient cetaceans by studying the fossils and bones they left behind, such as this dolphin skull.

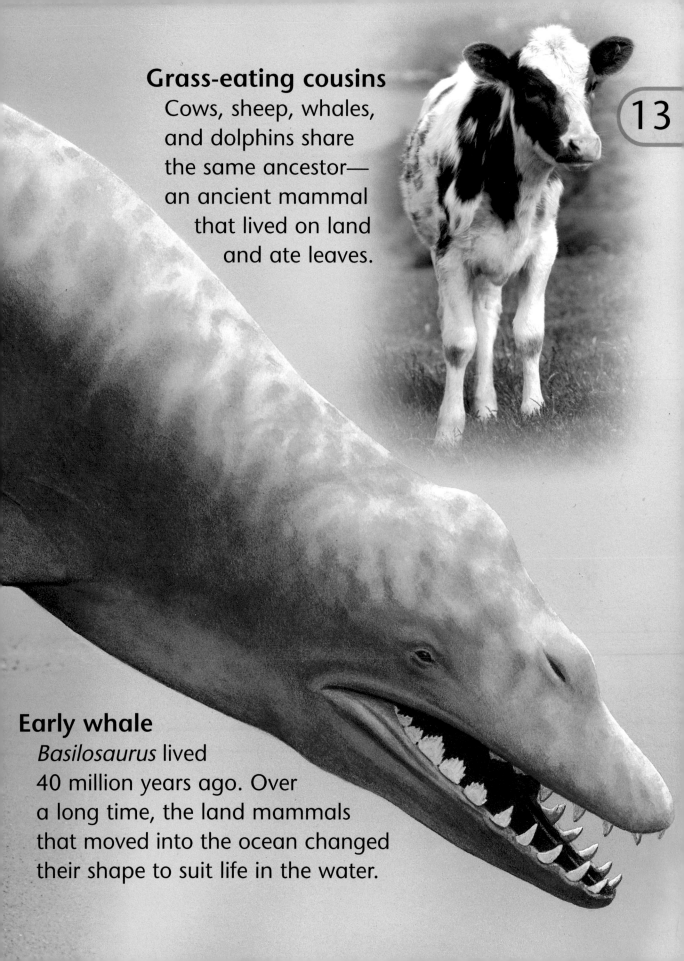

Grass-eating cousins

Cows, sheep, whales, and dolphins share the same ancestor— an ancient mammal that lived on land and ate leaves.

Early whale

Basilosaurus lived 40 million years ago. Over a long time, the land mammals that moved into the ocean changed their shape to suit life in the water.

Built for the sea

The long, smooth shape of cetaceans means that they are able to swim through water easily. Salty seawater is good at keeping heavy things buoyant, which is why whales can grow very large.

Full power

Instead of back legs, cetaceans have very strong tails with two flat paddles called flukes. Bottle-nosed dolphins can stand up using their tails alone.

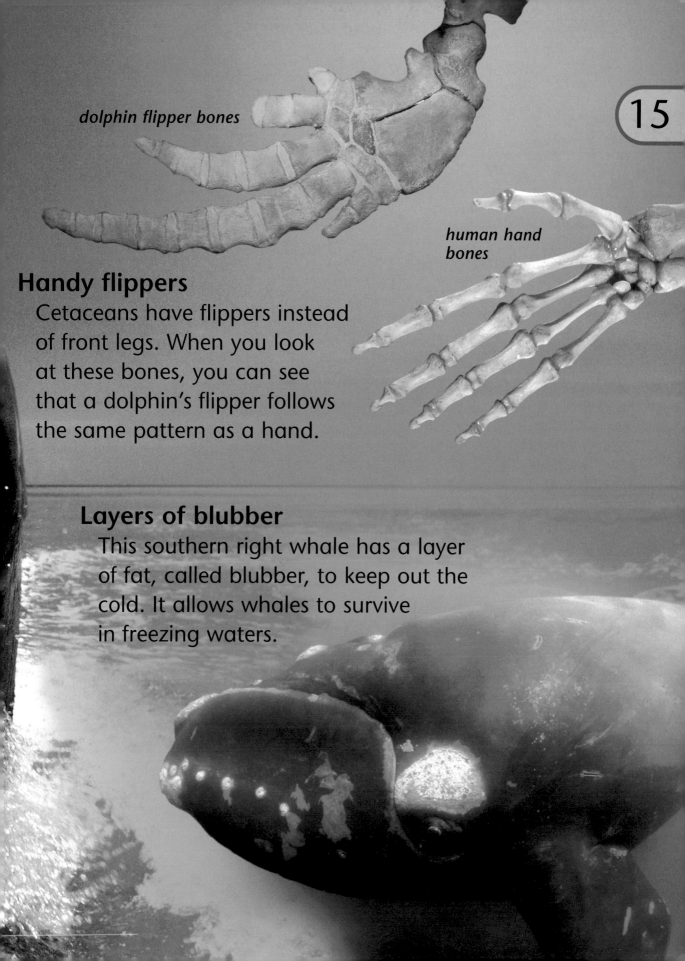

dolphin flipper bones

human hand bones

Handy flippers

Cetaceans have flippers instead of front legs. When you look at these bones, you can see that a dolphin's flipper follows the same pattern as a hand.

Layers of blubber

This southern right whale has a layer of fat, called blubber, to keep out the cold. It allows whales to survive in freezing waters.

Coming up **for air**

Like other mammals, whales and dolphins breathe using their lungs. They come to the water's surface to take in fresh air and blow out used air.

Deep down
Most whales can stay underwater for half an hour before needing to take a breath. Cetaceans take in air through a blowhole on the top of their head.

Blowing high

Many whales, such as this blue whale, have a double blowhole. The blowhole closes up when they dive so water will not get in.

Not the same

Dolphins have a single blowhole. The pattern of mist, called "blow," that sprays out is different for every species of cetacean.

Filter feeders

Cetaceans are split into two groups: those that have teeth and those that do not. The toothless whales, known as baleen whales, include humpbacks and grays. They feed by filtering tiny marine animals and small fish from the ocean.

What is baleen?

Instead of teeth, toothless whales have baleen—stiff, hairy sheets that hang in rows from their top jaws. Baleen traps food as water is filtered through it.

Big eaters

To eat enough food, humpbacks must gulp huge mouthfuls of water. Folds in their necks expand like a balloon to let in even more.

Clever hunters

All dolphins and porpoises and more than half of all whale species have teeth. They eat fish and larger sea creatures. Sperm whales love to eat giant squids.

Fearless predators

The orca, often called the killer whale, is actually a large dolphin. Its diet includes sea lions and even other cetaceans.

Open wide

A dolphin's teeth are used for grabbing, not chewing. Dolphins swallow their prey whole.

Teamwork

Bottle-nosed dolphins often hunt together. They surround groups of fish, sometimes driving them onto land and coming up halfway out of the water to grab them.

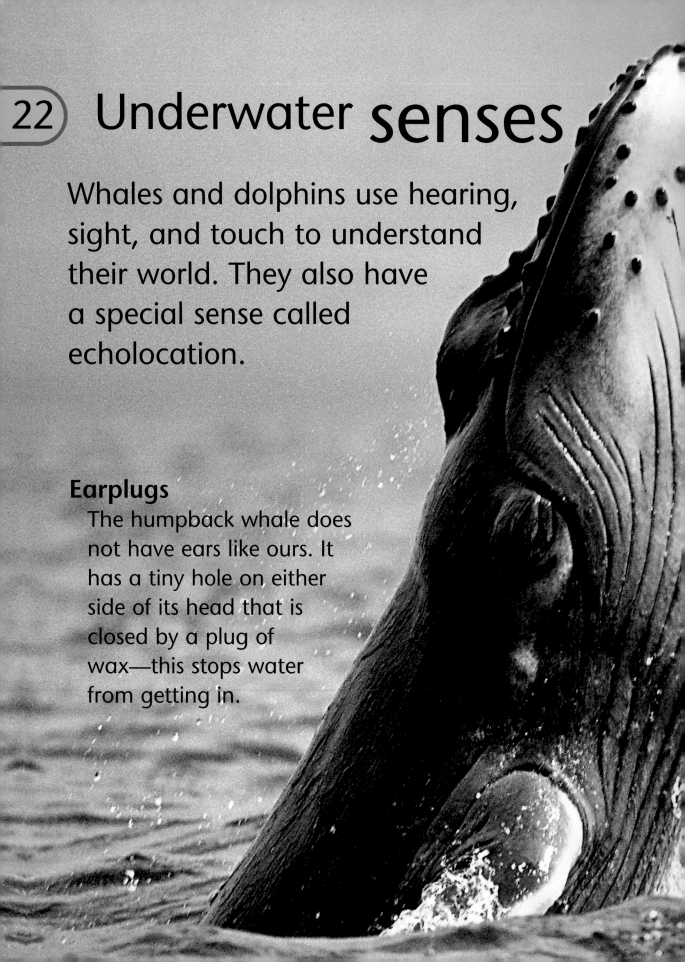

Underwater senses

Whales and dolphins use hearing, sight, and touch to understand their world. They also have a special sense called echolocation.

Earplugs

The humpback whale does not have ears like ours. It has a tiny hole on either side of its head that is closed by a plug of wax—this stops water from getting in.

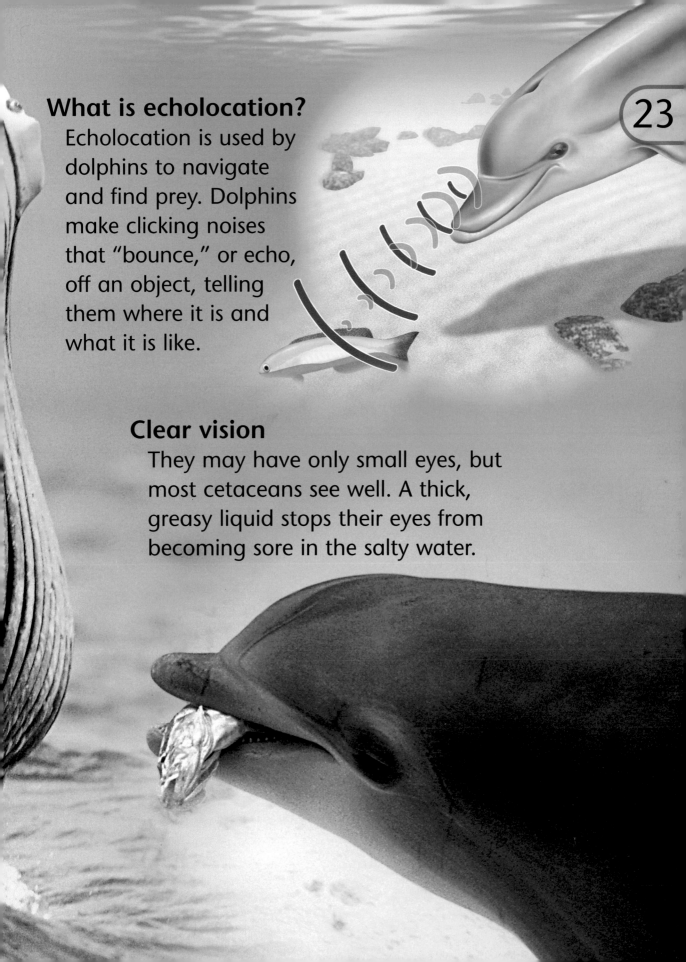

What is echolocation?

Echolocation is used by dolphins to navigate and find prey. Dolphins make clicking noises that "bounce," or echo, off an object, telling them where it is and what it is like.

Clear vision

They may have only small eyes, but most cetaceans see well. A thick, greasy liquid stops their eyes from becoming sore in the salty water.

Sea songs

All cetaceans use sounds to communicate. Baleen whales make low sounds, from loud grunts and squeals to bubbling noises. Dolphins whistle, squeak, and click.

Noisy neighbors

Dolphins make different noises for different reasons. Opening and shutting their mouths, called jaw clapping, is a sign that there may be a fight on the way.

The latest tune
Male humpbacks sing patterns of notes and sounds that can last up to half an hour.

Brainpower
Dolphins have large brains relative to the size of their bodies. They are fast learners and can even understand simple sentences.

Playing with waves

From slapping their fins and tails on the surface to spinning in the air, cetaceans display all kinds of behavior both above and below the water.

High fliers

Dusky dolphins are among the most acrobatic of all dolphins. They do breathtaking leaps and somersaults.

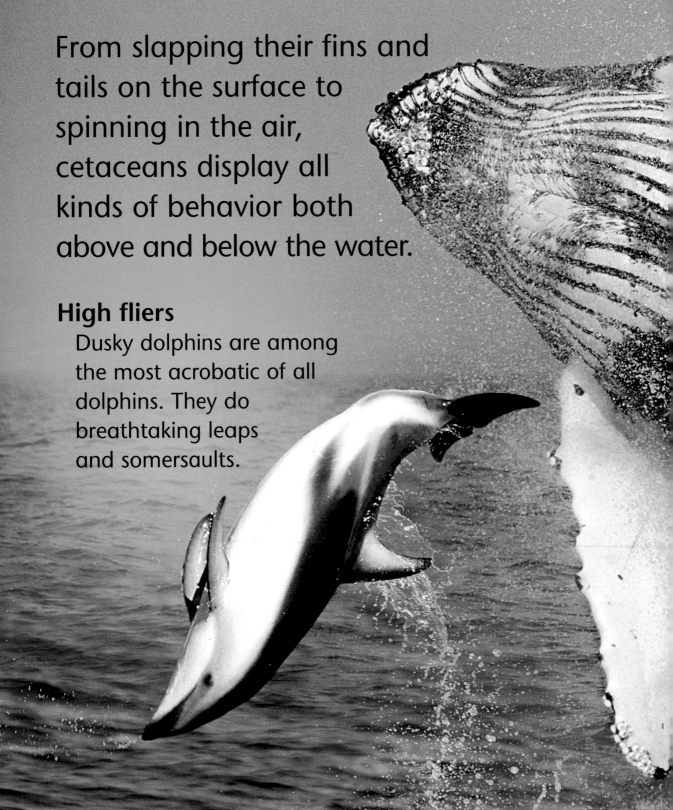

Who's there?
Killer whales spyhop, sticking their heads straight up out of the water, to spot penguins and seals on the ice.

A great sight
When whales launch themselves up out of the water, it is called breaching. Humpbacks have been seen breaching 100 times, over and over again.

Moving around

Whales travel, or migrate, between cold seas in the summer, where there is plenty of food, and warmer waters in the winter, where they have their families.

Record holders

Humpbacks and grays make the longest journeys. They can swim up to 9,950 miles (16,000 kilometers) in a year.

North America

South America

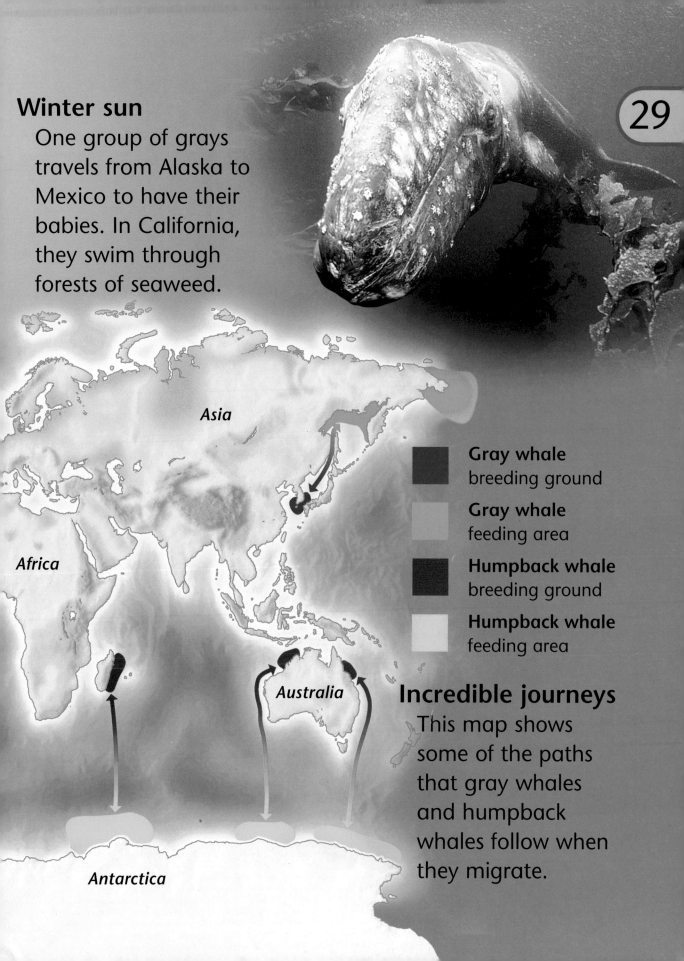

Winter sun

One group of grays travels from Alaska to Mexico to have their babies. In California, they swim through forests of seaweed.

Asia

Africa

Gray whale breeding ground

Gray whale feeding area

Humpback whale breeding ground

Humpback whale feeding area

Australia

Incredible journeys

This map shows some of the paths that gray whales and humpback whales follow when they migrate.

Antarctica

New lives

Whale and dolphin babies can swim as soon as they are born, but it takes many years until a calf is an adult.

Big babies
A humpback calf can measure one-third of its mother's length when it is born! It feeds on her milk for the first 11 months.

Long pregnancy

Dolphins can be pregnant for more than a year. The actual birth, however, is quick and may be over in less than an hour.

Staying close

Cetacean mothers stay close to their calves so they can protect them from predators.

Social animals

A group of cetaceans is known as a pod. Many pods are related, while others come together to feed or to protect their young.

Family ties

All the members of a killer whale pod are related to one original mother or grandmother. Killer whales usually stay with their families for life.

Will to win

Adult males often travel together. Male narwhals clash tusks to decide which will have the right to mate with a female.

Touchy-feely

Atlantic spotted dolphins are often seen in pods of about ten. Animals in these groups often nudge one another in a friendly way.

Making friends

People have always viewed dolphins as friendly creatures. Whales were once thought of as monsters, but today we want to protect them.

Watery friends

Swimming with dolphins has become popular with adults and children. Dolphins may even help people who are in trouble in the ocean.

Ancient links

This painting of dolphins is on a wall at the Palace of Knossos on the Greek island of Crete. It is 3,500 years old.

Big books

There are many stories about giant whales. In the Bible, Jonah was swallowed by a whale—and survived.

Human dangers

People can do things that harm cetaceans. For a long time, whales have been hunted for their meat, baleen, and blubber. Fishing nets and pollution are added dangers.

Whale rescue

Many dolphins and whales get caught and can die in fishing nets. This tangled-up sperm whale is being freed by a diver.

Under threat

The Chang Jiang (Yangtze River) in China is home to the baiji. This dolphin is endangered because the river is polluted.

Whaling ban
Whale hunting—known as whaling—has killed millions of cetaceans. Most countries have agreed to stop completely.

Growing knowledge

The more we learn about whales and dolphins, the more amazing we find they are. It is important to know as much as we can about them so that they can be better protected.

Getting to know them

Researchers can identify individual Risso's dolphins from the scars on their bodies. The pattern on each dolphin's body is different.

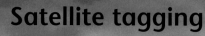

Satellite tagging

Cetaceans can now be followed from space! The tag on this beluga sends information to a satellite that can then track the beluga's location.

Looking and learning

There are chances to watch whales, dolphins, and porpoises in the wild throughout the world, from Ireland to the Caribbean and from Canada to Australia.

Free to roam
Today, there are a few cetacean sanctuaries. It is hoped that in the future there will be more.

Near the shore

Many species, especially
of dolphins, come close to
the coast. All you need
to spot them is a pair
of binoculars—and
some patience.

Thrilling sight

Special boat tours can give
great views. Responsible
tours do not crowd the
animals and make sure
they are not disturbed.

Leaping high

Hang this mobile in your bedroom, and you will have dolphins dancing before your eyes. Shiny paper makes them sparkle in the light.

You will need:
- Pencil
- Tracing paper
- Thin cardboard
- Scissors
- Modeling clay
- Compass
- Foil/shiny paper
- Glue
- Ruler
- Thick cardboard (12 in. x 12 in. or 30cm x 30cm)
- Ribbon

dolphin template

Decorate each dolphin with foil or shiny paper.

1

Trace the template and transfer the shape onto thin cardboard. Do this five times so that you have five dolphins. Cut out the dolphins.

2

Place modeling clay under the top fin of each dolphin shape. Using a compass, make a hole in each fin as shown.

Using a ruler, draw a line from the bottom-left corner of the thick cardboard to the top-right corner. Cut along the line to make two triangles and then decorate them.

Cut a notch halfway down the peak of one triangle. Next, cut a notch halfway up from the bottom of the other triangle. Make holes at the ends of each triangle.

dolphin mobile

Slot the triangles together to form the hanger. Make a hole where the two triangles meet at the bottom and another hole at the top.

Use ribbon to attach each dolphin to the hanger and then tie the knots. Pull ribbon through the hole at the top of the hanger to make a loop. You can now hang up your mobile.

Whale bookmark

Intelligent creatures

Cetaceans are among the smartest of all animals. Make markers in the shape of sea mammals to hold your place in favorite books.

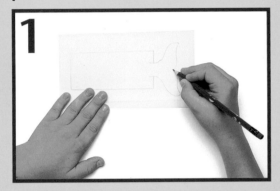

Measure a rectangle 2 in. x 6 in. (6cm x 15cm). Draw a whale's tail at one end of the shape. Draw waves where the tail meets the sea.

You will need:
- Cardboard
- Ruler
- Pencil
- Scissors
- Blue holographic paper
- Glue
- Markers
- Glitter pens

Cut out the bookmark, being careful to cut around the shape of the whale's tail and around the top of the waves.

Glue blue holographic paper to both sides of the bookmark for the sea. Use markers and glitter pens to color in the tail.

Does it float?

Testing buoyancy

When you put different items in water, some float on the surface and others sink to the bottom. Whales and dolphins need to come up for air, so they have to be buoyant enough not to sink straight down.

You will need:
- Large clear bowl
- Water
- Apple
- Stone
- Cork
- Ice cube

1 Think about the apple, stone, cork, and ice cube. Will they float or will they sink?

2 One by one, put each item into a bowl of water—were you right about which would float and which would sink?

Blue whale poster

Sea giants

Blue whales are the biggest animals on Earth. They can reach 108 feet (33 meters) long—the size of a large swimming pool. This project will give you an idea of just how big they are.

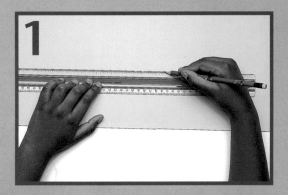

Using a ruler with centimeters on it, measure and mark a 30cm space, a 2cm space, an 8cm space, another 2cm space, and, finally, a 6cm space.

You will need:
- Large poster board
- Ruler
- Pencil
- Paints
- Paintbrush
- Tissue paper: green, blue, red
- Glue
- Cotton balls
- Scissors
- Gold holographic paper

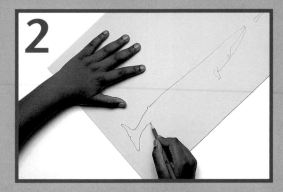

Draw a blue whale from tail to head in the 30cm space. Then draw a killer whale in the 8cm space and an elephant in the 6cm space.

Paint the blue whale, killer whale, and elephant, copying the colors and markings shown on the final picture on the opposite page.

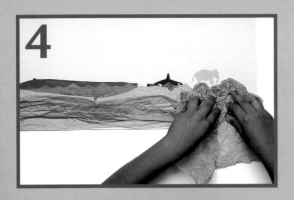

4

Decorate the picture with strips of tissue paper: green for land under the elephant and blue for water around the killer whale and blue whale.

5

Glue down cotton-balls for clouds. Then cut out a circle and eight strips of gold holographic paper and glue them down to make a Sun.

To finish your picture, twist some red tissue paper and glue it down to make a border. Now you can see how big a blue whale is!

Glossary

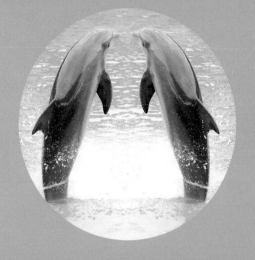

acrobatic—making movements that are difficult and skilled

ancestor—an animal from which later animals have developed

ancient—very old

baleen—the thin, hairy plates in a whale's mouth

behavior—how animals act

binoculars—an instrument with lenses for both eyes that you can use to see objects that are far away

blowhole—the airway through which whales, dolphins, and porpoises breathe

brain—the body part inside the head that is used to learn and think

breeding ground—a place where animals go to find a mate and have their young

buoyant—able to float in water

calf—a baby dolphin or whale

cetacean—the group name for whales, dolphins, and porpoises

coast—the area where the land meets the sea

communicate—to send a message to another creature

dive—to drop down headfirst

endangered—in danger of dying out

expand—to increase in size

fat—the soft, oily part under the skin of an animal

filtering—collecting tiny objects from the liquid (such as water) in which they are floating

fossil—evidence of a living thing from the past that is preserved in rock

identify—to recognize or name

journey—a long trip from one place to another

lungs—the parts inside the body that are used for breathing

mammal—a warm-blooded animal that feeds its young milk

marine—having to do with the sea

navigate—to find your way around

patience—the ability to wait for a long time for something to happen

pattern—if things are in a pattern, then they are put together in a similar way

pollution—harmful waste

popular—liked by a lot of people

predator—an animal that hunts and eats other animals

pregnancy—the period of time when a baby grows inside its mother

prey—an animal that is killed and eaten by another animal

protect—to prevent something or someone from being harmed

related—being part of the same family

responsible—a responsible person behaves properly, without having to be supervised

sanctuary—a safe place, protected from harm by humans

satellite—a spacecraft that orbits Earth

scar—a mark left on the skin after a cut has healed

social—living in a group

somersault—a forward or backward roll where the body is brought over the head

species—a set of animals or plants with the same features

squid—a sea creature with a long, soft body and many tentacles

tropical—an area near the equator where it is hot all year long

unicorn—a mythical animal like a horse with a long horn

wax—an oily material in the ear that protects it

The content of this book can be used to teach, reinforce, and enhance many components of the science and language arts curricula. This high-interest topic is well suited for numerous crosscurricular connections, particularly in math, geography, and art.

Extension activities

Language arts
Writing
1) Use this book and other references to create your own book about cetaceans. Write about a different type of cetacean on each page with an illustration and two to three paragraphs of information.

2) The long tusk of a narwhal may be where stories about unicorns began (p. 11). Write a fantasy story about a narwhal and its adventures.

Speaking and listening
Cetaceans communicate using sounds (pp. 24–25). With a friend, develop a language of sounds and tunes, but no words. Practice and demonstrate your language.

Using graphic organizers
Cetaceans share certain characteristics with all mammals, but they are very different in some ways, too. Use a Venn diagram to show the similarities and differences between cetaceans and bears.

Science
The study of whales and dolphins relates to scientific themes of diversity, structure and function, adaptations, growth and development, interdependence, and interaction with the environment. Some specific links to science curriculum content include characteristics of mammals (pp. 6–7, 16–17); classification (pp. 6–9, 13, 18–19, 38); adaptations (pp. 8–11, 14–23); habitats (pp. 8–10, 14, 16); food chains and webs (pp. 18–21); predator/prey relationships (pp. 18–21, 27); behavior (pp. 8–30, 34); reproduction (pp. 6–7, 30–31); senses (pp. 22–23); communication (pp. 22–25); and conservation (pp. 34, 36–41).

Crosscurricular links
1) *Math/measurement:* a blue whale (p. 11) can reach 110 feet

(33 meters, or 37 yards) in length. Measure and draw a chalk line this long on a sidewalk or blacktop. Have someone help you mark segments along the line the same length as your height.

2) *Math/graphing:* research to find the lengths of at least five cetacean species. Show your data on a bar graph or line graph. Extension: make similar graphs for other characteristics such as weight or life span.

3) *Geography:* some types of cetaceans are found all over the world. Others live only in certain regions. Use the map on pp. 28–29 to locate the home or range of as many different species as you can.

Using the projects
Children can do these projects at home. Here are some ideas for extensions:

Pages 42–43: Model each dolphin after a different species. Write a short report about each one and put them together to make a book.

Page 44: Find out about other sea mammals in addition to cetaceans. Make bookmarks to add to your sea mammal collection.

Page 45: Most cetaceans live in salt water (p. 14). Fill another bowl with water. Stir in one cup of salt. Compare how each item floats in salt water and fresh water. Try using other objects such as a raw egg or an orange.

Pages 46–47: A humpback whale is about half the length of a blue whale. A bottle-nosed dolphin is about half the length of a killer whale. Draw these animals to the same scale and add them to your picture.

Did you know?

- Dolphins can swim up to 850 feet (260 meters) below the surface of the ocean.

- Dolphins can stay underwater for up to 15 minutes. Sperm whales can stay underwater for as long as 90 minutes.

- The largest dolphin is the orca, also known as the "killer whale."

- A bottle-nosed dolphin's brain weighs between 53 and 56 ounces. That's the same as one and a half bags of sugar.

- Dolphins can jump as high as 20 feet (6 meters) out of the water.

- Male whales use their singing voices to try to attract females during the mating season.

- Whales breathe air like we do. They need to reach the surface of the ocean in order to take in air through their blowhole.

- Whales can swim as fast as 30 miles per hour (48 kilometers per hour). The fastest human sprinter can run at 22 miles per hour (36 kilometers per hour).

- Whales and dolphins do not sleep like we do. They rest only half of their brain at a time. The other half continues to operate. Otherwise, they would stop breathing and drown.

- Male dolphins are called bulls, and female dolphins are called cows.

- Scientists have discovered that dolphins are as smart as human toddlers. They are capable of recognizing their own reflections in the mirror.

- Female killer whales have been known to live for up to 80 years.

- Dolphins make loud clicking sounds to stun any small fish in range. Then they eat them.

- A dolphin's extremely long jaws may contain as many as 250 pointy white teeth. That would keep a dentist very busy!

- The deepest dive by a bottle-nosed dolphin ever recorded is about 985 feet (300 meters). This was made by a dolphin trained by the U.S. Navy.

- Dolphins look like they are smiling all the time even if they are sick or injured. This is because they cannot move the muscles in their faces.

- A blue whale calf weighs 2 tons at birth. That is the same as two large horses!

- An adult blue whale's heart weighs as much as a small car.

- Mother dolphins have babysitters for their young. The dolphins' "sisters" help the mother during the birth of her young. Sister dolphins also stay close to help with babysitting.

- Dolphin calves are born tail first so that they do not drown. Their mother quickly pushes them up to the surface of the water for their first breath.

- Dolphins have two stomachs—one for storing food and one for digesting it.

- A dolphin's skin is very sensitive and is easily injured by rough surfaces—a lot like human skin.

- Dolphins are not only found in oceans—some species live in rivers. Amazon dolphins (botos) are a type of river dolphin. They are born gray, but they grow pink with age!

The answers to these questions can all be found by looking back through the book. See how many you get right. You can check your answers on page 56.

1) What is a baby dolphin called?
   A—a calf
   B—a pup
   C—a foal

2) The short-beaked common dolphin likes . . .
   A—cold water
   B—warm water
   C—freezing water

3) How long can a male narwhal's tusk reach?
   A—3 feet (1 meter)
   B—6.5 feet (2 meters)
   C—10 feet (3 meters)

4) Dolphins are . . .
   A—fish
   B —mammals
   C—amphibians

5) What do cetaceans have instead of front legs?
   A—flippers
   B—arms
   C—tusks

6) How does a dolphin breathe?
   A—through its blowhole
   B—through its nose
   C—through its mouth

7) What do toothless whales have instead of teeth?
   A—gums
   B—baleen
   C—fangs

8) What is another name for an orca?
   A—fish
   B—squid
   C—killer whale

9) What stops dolphins' eyes from getting sore from the salty water in the ocean?
   A—wax
   B—a thick, greasy liquid
   C—blood

10) Dolphins can . . .
   A—count
   B—dance
   C—understand simple sentences

11) What is it called when whales launch themselves up out of the water?
   A—jumping
   B—breaching
   C—flying

12) Researchers can identify individual Risso's dolphins from . . .
   A—their flippers
   B—the scars on their bodies
   C—their eyes

Books to read

The Best Book of Whales and Dolphins by Christiane Gunzi, Kingfisher, 2006

Explorers: Oceans and Seas by Stephen Savage, Kingfisher, 2010

Weird Ocean by Kathryn Smith, Kingfisher, 2010

Whales and Dolphins by Susanna Davidson, Usborne Books, 2009

Wild World: Watching Dolphins in the Oceans by Elizabeth Miles, Heinemann-Raintree, 2005

Places to visit

Seaworld, Orlando, Florida
www.seaworld.com
Discover marine animals up close, from emperor penguins and rescued sea turtles to killer whales, plus newborn dolphins in the Dolphin Nursery.

Hyannis Whale Watcher Cruises, Barnstable, Massachusetts
www.whales.net/index.html
Join in Cape Cod's whale-watching experience for a chance to catch a glimpse of these majestic creatures spyhopping, flipping, and playing, plus learn more about whales' habitats and behavior and the importance of conservation.

Discovery Cove, Orlando, Florida
www.discoverycove.com
Swim with the dolphins or snorkel in a tropical reef full of colorful fish and manta rays.

Websites

www.kids.nationalgeographic.com
Learn about bottle-nosed dolphins, orcas, and whales with facts, photos, videos, and games to play.

www.nhm.ac.uk
With a section just for children, there are games to play, pictures, and videos to watch. You can also learn about people who study whales and dolphins as their career.

www.dolphins-world.com
Find out more about dolphins and whales with coloring pages, three-dimensional puzzles, and pictures that help you learn about these fascinating animals.

www.sheddaquarium.org
Watch video clips of a beluga whale calf at the Shedd Aquarium's website.

Whales and dolphins
quiz answers

1) A   7) B
2) B   8) C
3) C   9) B
4) B   10) C
5) A   11) B
6) A   12) B